The Occul Syst

CW00449988

UFOs, aliens, other dimensions, and future timelines

By Daniel Pinchbeck

ISBN 9781080888467

CONTENTS

1 FROM THE PERIPHERY TO THE CENTER

All of a sudden, the mainstream media has turned its focus on the subject of UFOs, a global phenomenon they have derided and dismissed until now. The tone has shifted drastically in recent articles in The New York Times and Washington Post, partly due to 'Unidentified', a new series on the History Channel. The series exhaustively chronicles military encounters with what appear to be diverse alien craft. The Times reports on myriad anomalies encountered by pilots as recently as 2015, including a report of an object akin to a "spinning top moving against the wind" and another "like a sphere encasing a cube." These objects were able to accelerate to hypersonic speeds, make sudden stops and instantaneous turns with no visible engine or exhaust plumes. For some conspiracy theorists, the new spate of articles suggests we are approaching a threshold of disclosure - the long-awaited release of withheld information on UFOs and ETs. It is also possible that this partial disclosure has been orchestrated by intelligence agencies whose motives remain opaque and unclear.

Whatever the truth, the issue of UFOs and the alien presence is steadily moving from the outer edge or periphery of public awareness toward the center. I would like to explore why this is happening and what it means. I will also consider what we could and perhaps should do, individually and collectively, in response.

I enjoy observing the process as once-esoteric topics

spiral from the edge of collective awareness toward the center. Over the last decades, another formerly taboo subject followed a similar path - namely, psychedelics. Before I published my book on psychedelic shamanism, *Breaking Open the Head*, in 2002, you simply could not speak about psychedelic exploration in a city like New York or London, if you wanted to be known as a serious, respectable person in the media or the arts. When I tried to broach the subject at a social gathering of journalists, art world aficionados, or literary writers, the response would be ridicule and curt dismissal. Psychedelics seemed caught in a double bind of repression: Most people not only had a knee-jerk negative reaction to it, but they were also unable to consider why they felt the need to repress any interest in the subject so intensely. This remains the situation today, when it comes to UFOs and the question of alien contact.

The culture has lifted its interdiction on psychedelics. They are now fashionable objects of fascination - promoted in bestselling books, TV shows, and numerous documentaries. Today we find ourselves in a full-fledged psychedelic renaissance with amazing research happening across the world. This is a great development - it also suggests that a similar reversal might happen when it comes to other prohibited areas of inquiry, such as the still forbidden topics of UFOs, alien abductions, and other-dimensional visitors.

What prevents the UFO and alien topic from becoming culturally acceptable is that we lack a framework for understanding it or giving it meaning. It remains unpresentable, unfathomable. If we are going to assimilate it - and perhaps even neutralize the implicitly threatening aspects of it - we must develop a narrative and define a philosophical and conceptual model that gives shape and coherence to the phenomenon. With this essay, I hope to assist in this difficult task of discernment.

Dismissiveness and derision have been the dominant response to the subject of UFOS and alien abductions - also crop circles, a subject I explored in depth in my book, *2012: The Return of Quetzalcoatl* - for decades. The thousands-upon-thousands of sightings of strange craft by ordinary people as well as trained military personnel, the vast numbers of bewildering and terrifying abduction stories, the aesthetically profound, precise, and gargantuan crop circles that still appear in UK wheat fields every summer with no explanation - none of this has made any difference until now. These topics fall so far outside of mainstream discourse that you cannot explore them without risking exile to the dismissible, lunatic fringe. Journalists and academics who pursue this inquiry with some level of objectivity and rigor find themselves thrown out of the establishment, forced to build alternative structures to circulate their ideas. In my case, I wrote one article for *Wired Magazine* on the crop circles in 2002, leaving open the possibility that it wasn't entirely a hoax. After the publication, the editor-in-chief was appalled. I was never able to write for *Wired* again.

The reasons for this blockade are, I think, obvious. The main function of mainstream discourse is not to excavate uncomfortable truth but to preserve and protect the status quo. Popular media and academia constantly seek to establish a boundary - a bulwark or line of defense - inside of which society can continue comfortably, without disruption. Most people innately seek and unconsciously wish to remain oblivious to anything that might threaten the belief system they are trying to maintain, which gives them a sense of security and stability.

Our culture still holds to the secular materialist paradigm developed during the Renaissance, the Enlightenment, and through the Scientific and Industrial Revolutions. Even though contemporary physics defined a radically different view of the nature of reality from that of Newton, people still believe themselves safely anchored in the Newtonian/Cartesian universe, where matter has solidity and consciousness only exists due to the biological hardware of the brain.

I believe this self-protective herd instinct, rejecting any difficult material that pushes people outside of their ideological comfort zone, is a danger to our future. It is not farfetched to say this habit may contribute to our extinction in the near term. We see the same tendency to avoid and distract when it comes to climate change and the ecological emergency that is on the verge of engulfing us. Even among the privileged and intellectual elite, most people, at this point, lack the initiative as well as the courage to explore and assimilate a lot of the crucial data - let alone take it to heart and act upon it.

With the ecological crisis, it is not a case of confronting bizarre and ineffable evidence, as with alien abductions and UFOs, or even psychedelic hallucinations. The scientific data is merciless and clear. We know we are tearing apart the biospheric support systems of the Earth. Yet only children are still awake and aware enough to realize that something must be done about it. Teenagers have started taking to the streets in vast numbers, leaving the adults - their supposed protectors - far behind in their gape-jawed stupidity.

There is, I believe, an intrinsic connection between our failure to address these particular areas - aliens, psychedelics, the ecological emergency - that society has avoided and pushed to the periphery. Taken seriously, these subjects threaten the foundation, the underlying paradigm, of contemporary civilization. (As a side note, while our culture has assimilated the healing aspect of psychedelics over the last decade, it has sidestepped the more ontologically difficult aspects of the experience, such as psychic and psycho-physical manifestations, as well as the abrupt breach into other dimensions of reality that can be both fascinating and frightening.) On the one hand, self-repression and self-censorship are habitual. Our society normalizes this tendency. You are only meant to be cognizant of a narrow bandwidth of ideas and information, and not step into the unknown.

On a larger level, it seems like some spell has been cast over humanity as a whole, trapping us in an energetic frequency of limitation. As we will explore, it seems there is something like an occult control system that operates invisibly. This system expertly exploits our cognitive biases and psychological blindspots to keep humanity, as a whole, ignorant, docile and subordinate. If somebody or some group begins to penetrate its defenses and expose it, they often get attacked in various ingenious ways. The control system finds and exploits their character flaws, targeting the chinks in their armor. If we can entertain such a hypothesis, we might then inquire into the reasons for this matrix-like control system, how it functions, and how it could be overcome.

Many of us sense, inchoately, that the period we are in now is something like an interregnum - a calm before the storm. So many changes are happening so rapidly that it is almost impossible to keep track of all of them. Not too long ago, neoliberal academics confidently proclaimed we had attained the "end of history" in a stable geopolitical order that would plod along forever, increasingly bringing the comforts of a corporate hyper-consumerist monoculture to everyone. But history came roaring back with a vengeance.

Today we have a far Right Wing uprising in many parts of the world, increasing numbers of refugees (65 million with more on the way), corruption of the information sphere with "fake news", internment camps in the US where migrant children are senselessly tormented, and so on. The rapid development of technology, driven by profit-seeking corporations, is also unleashing unpredictable, destabilizing effects. According to a recent UN report, global civilization has less than a decade to radically reduce CO_2 consumption or face catastrophic failure. We do not seem to be rallying to accomplish that goal. There is a sense, as in WB Yeats' poem, that "the center cannot hold."

At this turbulent juncture, one might wonder, why is it so difficult for humans to get our act together? What is it that smashes apart all of our efforts to establish better, more humane and coherent societies and systems? Why are we moving backward, regressing, when our creative and technical capacities and authentic prospects seem greater than ever?

It seems an invisible *something* presses down on us, contorting all of our efforts, so that our best intentions lead to the worst outcomes or the repetition of old miseries. Of course, most would argue that this force is simply human greed and ignorance - and they may be correct. But perhaps other forces are at play as well. Perhaps there are, indeed "off planet," "extra-" or "infra-dimensional" entities manipulating humanity, seeking to advance their own agendas. To be honest, I am quite certain this is the case.

I have met a number of disinterested skeptics who changed their minds after delving into evidence as well as reading many personal accounts. In some cases, they find their belief system shaken to the core. Many former military personnel and intelligence agents have privately admitted knowledge of the phenomenon, as well as fear of the mysterious power behind it. At this point, there is an onslaught of reports of craft eluding fighter jets, performing impossible maneuvers, moving at 25,000 miles per hour, suddenly splitting into two, vanishing entirely, and also hovering over nuclear bases to deactivate missile guidance systems, seemingly with no problem.

Certain factions within the military and military intelligence, it seems, take seriously the prospect that these aliens may be preparing to attack us. Former Democratic Senate Majority Leader Harry Reid has stated that the US is currently competing with the USSR and China to investigate UFO activity, and, potentially, to learn what they can about "breakthrough" aerospace technology that seems centuries ahead of our own. It also seems increasingly likely that former US governments have indeed communicated with some of the alien groups, in some form or another, going back decades.

According to some insiders, there are different cabals within the military and intelligence agencies. Some of these groups seek public disclosure and some fight against it. Apparently, there are people working within this apparatus who believe the alien presence is not just otherworldly, but extends from a different space-time dimension. According to numerous accounts, there appear to be different alien groups, with varied agendas.

This is, in essence, the conclusion reached by historian Richard Dolan, whose authoritative two-volume treatise,

UFOS and the National Security State, traces US Government knowledge and involvement with UFOs and possibly ETs from the 1940s to recent times. Of anyone who has devoted his career to studying this phenomenon, Dolan seems the most credible and scrupulous researcher. As an academically trained historian, he remains dubious of many claims made by others in the UFO community, such as David Wilcock and Corey Goode, who, he insinuates, may themselves be agents of disinformation. Yet he has gone far down the rabbit hole in his efforts to comprehend the vast weirdness - the high strangeness - of the UFO and alien abduction phenomenon.

In fact, based on decades of assiduous and careful research, Dolan paints a picture of a looking-glass reality, astonishingly different from what we - even those of us who pay attention to undercurrents of geopolitics and New World Order conspiracies - think we know. He believes there is an elite group within the private sector as well the military that has excavated alien craft, performed autopsies on alien bodies, and gained the capacity to make use of alien technology. He calls this secret cabal a "breakaway civilization," which has evolved, in its technical capacities, far beyond the rest of us. Among the secrets they are holding are energy technologies that would make fossil fuels obsolete - and irrevocably alter the balance of power in the world.

Dolan argues that the US government began its UFO coverup in the late 1940s and has continued ever since. In 1947, thousands of sightings of alien craft occurred in the US. It was headline news across the country. In that same year, the infamous Roswell crash occurred in New Mexico. According to Wikipedia, this incident was merely a crashed weather balloon. However, most UFO researchers believe it was far more than that. There have been testimonies from people involved in the aftermath of the crash, among other evidence. Of course, such testimonies could also be disinformation.

In *The Secret Space Program*, Dolan writes, "We have had retrievals of exotic technologies and bodies. I believe they were extraterrestrial." Dolan writes that Russia and China also pursue this subject actively, and, most probably, have also recovered alien craft and bodies. He thinks that the wall of secrecy around aliens and UFOs incited the rampant post-war growth of a vast apparatus of military intelligence aimed at controlling the flow of information as well as society itself.

The alien presence is, for Dolan, the "great secret" behind all of the other secrets and lies told by the world's governments. Personally, I don't necessarily agree with all of Dolan's conclusions - mainly because, as we will explore, I think he takes an approach that is a bit too literal-minded, materialist, and dualistic. However, what he is doing - exploring the subject through a carefully reasoned, evidence-based lens - is necessary. I see the need for a multidimensional approach, sometimes known as Ariadne's thread, utilizing every form of logic, intuition, and metaphysical speculation we can bring to this area, so we can define the solution sets to the deeply troubling questions that he, as well as others, have raised.

2. THE SUN OF DARKNESS

I began with the notion that, as a culture or a civilization, we are undergoing a polarity switch between what we consider central or essential, and what we find to be peripheral or unimportant. The center and the periphery are, in other words, changing places. This is part of a larger epochal shift that we can best understand through a mythological and cosmological lens. In the simplest terms, the polarity switch is between prioritizing the material and seemingly objective external reality or the internal dimensions of consciousness and subjective awareness.

Sergio Magana is a Nahuatl, Aztec, Nagual (sorcerer) from Mexico whose books include *The Dawn of the Sixth Sun*. Magana was trained by Nahuatl elders in Mexico City and carries their ancient knowledge forward into today's world. According to this tradition, we are currently in a transition between what they call a "Sun of Light" and a "Sun of Darkness." These transitions happen every 5,000 years or so, as our Solar System passes through different regions of the galaxy.

Magana's perspective aligns with the Long Count calendar of the classical Maya, a 5,125 year cycle that ended on December 21, 2012. He believes that 2012 - 2021 represents the in-between phase as we transition from a Sun of Light to one of Darkness. During a Sun of Light, humanity explores the material and physical world, the exterior, or surface dimension. This includes materialist science and rational logic. As we plunge into a Sun of

Darkness, however, we collectively dive back into the more evanescent realm of the dreamworld, into the shifting, shimmering waters of the Psyche. Reality, itself, becomes more psychically malleable; the world becomes increasingly like a waking dream. For those who don't have an esoteric worldview, such a shift can be deeply destabilizing and disorienting, even fatally so.

Personally, I believe we find indications all around us that this shift is underway. I did my best to chronicle the subtle, multidimensional and psychic nature of this ongoing transition in my book, *2012: The Return of Quetzalcoatl*. Unfortunately, the mass media ignored the nuances of my arguments, trying instead to "kill the messenger." I was tarred as a "doomsday" thinker, when my work stated the opposite. By seeking to raise consciousness, I was doing what I could to avert the catastrophic consequences of continued ignorance and inaction. Getting misconstrued in this way was both painful and instructive.

From our current vantage point, I do think we can acknowledge a profound, still-deepening shift in the collective field of both the outer and inner worlds over the last decade. Everything has changed to such a degree that even the recent past seems sepia-toned, vaguely inaccessible. It is as if we have entered a different frequency, or in the esoteric philosopher GI Gurdjieff's term, "octave," of consciousness. It almost seems like humanity, as a whole, has embarked on a prolonged psychedelic trip together - a journey that may lead, eventually, into entirely unforeseen or previously concealed regions or dimensions of being.

What Karl Marx once noted about the innate tendency of modernity - "all that is solid melts into air" - now seems true across the board. Our environmental support systems, to take one example, have been destabilized to such a degree that all future bets are off. The global financial meltdown of 2008 revealed our economic system to be fragile and based upon collective faith, above all. Since then we have seen the rise of blockchain-based currencies able to generate vast fortunes for private companies and individuals, without any known utility. An ongoing breakdown of outmoded patriarchal structures is underway as women join forces, amplifying their voices through the Internet. At the same time we witness the rise of "fake news" which impacts popular opinion and elections, and the new threat of "deep fakes," doctored video and audio that can convincingly show any person saying or doing anything. Then there is Artificial Intelligence, CRISPR, three-dimensional printing, new technologies capable of reading our thoughts, total surveillance systems, and so on.

The felt sense that we have moved from a time of relative clarity to one of murky ambiguity, confusion and corruption is, of course, exemplified by Trump's Presidency as well as the rise of the Alt Right. In many respects, Trump's ascendancy has a dream-like, surreal quality to it. Trump himself seems a liminal, trickster, or Loki-like figure - akin to the Lord of Misrule from a fairy tale. The Trump card in the deck is the one that automatically and arbitrarily wins over all of the others. Symbolically, this reflects the impermeable psychic field surrounding his meteoric rise as well as his astounding capacity to shrug off scandals that would have annihilated any previous president many times over. Trump has trumped the system. With his victory, it feels we have fully entered the realm of the hyper-real or what the French philosopher Jean Baudrillard called the Simulacrum.

As monstrous as Trump is, I personally don't think Obama was much different or better - something I argue, interminably, with impassioned liberals. I ignored the far-out (but entertaining) conspiracy theories that Obama was cloned either from the Egyptian Pharaoh Akhenaton or Malcolm X. At the same time, I found something almost too perfect about him. He seemed a precision instrument, perfectly crafted to maintain the New World Order, placating minorities and the underclass, at a particular historical juncture. Despite his enticing rhetoric, he faithfully served the fossil fuel interests, Wall Steel, and the military industrial complex.

I recall, just five days before Obama's January 2009 inauguration, there was the "miracle on the Hudson." As an article in The Conversation reminds us, "Captain Chesley "Sully" Sullenberger landed an Airbus A320-214 in New York's freezing Hudson River following a bird strike-induced loss of both engines. All 155 passengers and crew on board US Airways Flight 1549 survived." This heroic act seemed a dreamlike projection of the collective yearning to believe in Obama as the good captain who would pilot the SS America to a safe landing.

Of course, the Swiss psychoanalyst Carl Jung did the most, in the twentieth century, to reveal the dream-like nature of reality, which he saw expressing itself through synchronicities that reveal the bridge between mind and matter, as well as archetypal symbols and processes that unfold through both the individual and collective Psyche. Jung's last book, *The Flying Saucer Myth*, focused on the epidemic of UFO sightings in the years following the end of World War Two. Noting the round shape of the saucers, Jung interpreted them as symbols of psychic wholeness - like the center of the mandala around which the Psyche spirals in dreams. He proposed that the prevalence of UFO sightings suggested we were approaching the crescendo of the Apocalypse. The word "Apocalypse" means uncovering, revealing; the "unveiling of the hidden thing." For Jung, the inner meaning of the Apocalypse was not destruction but "the coming of the Self into conscious realization" - the incarnation of the complete human personality, comprising both dark and light, unconscious and conscious, elements.

In fact, until this point, the most compelling thinkers on the phenomenon of UFOs, Extra- or Infra-Terrestrials, and abductions have applied a psychological, psychic, or mythological perspective, rather than a literal one. UFOlogist Jacques Vallee linked alien abductions to ancient folktales in which humans trespassed or were cajoled into the realm of the fairy folk. He found these episodes belonged to "the domain of the in-between, the unproven, and the unprovable, . . . the country of paradoxes, strangely furnished with material 'proofs,' sometimes seemingly unimpeachable, but always ultimately insufficient. . . . This absolutely confusing (and manifestly misleading) aspect . . . may well be the phenomenon's most basic characteristic." He examined many accounts of abductions by faeries in the Middle Ages and noted that the contemporary accounts simply substitute a kind of faceless technological matrix for the more baroque aesthetics of the faery world.

A brilliant chronicler of the realms of the soul, the alchemical imagination, and the otherworld which he calls the "daimonic reality," Patrick Harpur explores extraterrestrials and the abduction phenomenon through a framework that deconstructs our modern literalism which he finds flawed and limited. "We cannot see the world except through some perspective or imaginal framework -

in short, some myth," he writes in *The Philosopher's Secret Fire*. "Indeed, the world we see is the myth we are in." We easily forget that our model of the world is just one way of relating to reality, one picture or idea - one myth. Literalism, in particular, blinds us from being able to envision the multiple or even myriad levels of reality that may exist simultaneously.

Even the apparent solidity of our physical bodies do not support the literal worldview, according to Harpur: "Outside Christendom, and other monotheistic religions, the soul is as quasi-material as the body is quasi-spiritual - both forming a daimonic whole. We are fluid organisms, passing easily between this world and the other, between life and death." Western occultists tend to substantiate the idea of a "subtle body," etheric or astral, which they differentiate from the physical. But traditional cultures, Harpur notes, do not "take this sort of body too literally… It is more usual - almost universal outside our culture - to understand that the physical body is also 'subtle' and that it can therefore easily be taken into the Otherworld because it is not in the first instance a literal thing." This is an extraordinary idea - quite difficult for the modern Western mind to accept.

For Harpur, the alien visitors, whether in mysterious craft able to violate laws of gravity or in abduction accounts that are often absurdly Kafkaesque, express this daimonic reality, the in-between realm of the soul, which slips through the planes of reality and illusion, unable to be defined or mentally categorized. "Daimons tend to disregard causality just as they ignore other laws, such as space and time, that we are pleased to impose on a world whose reality is quite otherwise," he notes. As an expression of this Daimonic reality, however, the Grey aliens - removing people from their lives in a trance-like paralysis, performing operations on them, subjecting them to various cruel torments - seem particularly demonic.

3. THE ABDUCTION AGENDA

The abduction phenomenon has changed and evolved over time. It has gone through a number of phases since the initial reports in the 1950s and early '60s. Most commonly, the aliens responsible for taking humans into their otherworldly craft and performing experiments on them are the ones known in popular culture as the Greys. The appearance and behavior of the Greys became more uniform over the course of decades. In the 1950s, many people reported encountering saucers with little spacemen working on them, but these figures did not conform to the description we now know. Abductees often meet other alien beings as well, such as tall blond "Nordics", also "reptilians," and occasionally, insectile entities. The descriptions of these beings tend to have a bizarre, cartoonish quality, which adds to the difficulty people have in taking the subject seriously.

In *Close Encounters of the Fourth Kind* (1995), *New Yorker* contributor C. D. B. Bryan crafted a physical portrait of the visitors, exploring their many anomalies. "The aliens' bodies are flat, paunchless. Their chests are not bifurcated; they have no nipples. Nor does the chest swell or diminish with breathing," he wrote. Many researchers believe the Greys to be more like clones or machines, powered in some way we cannot comprehend, as they do not seem to eat, drink, or excrete.

David Jacobs' *The Threat: Revealing the Secret Alien Agenda* (1999) is a frightening account of the abduction phenomenon. A hypnotherapist and professor of history at

Temple University, Jacobs believes that, after years of working with abductees, he distilled a logical and entirely horrifying picture of what the Grays are doing. He believes they are planning a takeover of the Earth, substituting a new hybrid human-alien species for the Earth's current inhabitants, at a threshold of global catastrophe.

During abductions, captured humans are often forced to undergo surgical procedures or participate in a hybrid alien breeding program, getting eggs and sperm removed. In some accounts, the aliens bring hybrid alien babies to female abductees, informing them that this is their child. Sometimes abductees are also made to play with hybrid alien children, described as melancholy or lethargic. The hybrid children play with blocks, similar to the blocks used by human children. But the alien blocks do not have letters or numbers on them—instead, they emit different emotions when they are turned. Since they are telepathic, the visitors have no need to learn spelling or counting. The toys seem to indicate, instead, that they are trying to learn how to feel - or at least to imitate human reactions.

During the encounters recovered in Jacobs's hypnotherapy sessions, abductees are often shown scenes, like propaganda films, of an apocalyptic event—nuclear war or sudden climate change—in the near-future, followed by clips of hybrid human-aliens walking arm in arm across a transformed Earth, the sun shining down on them peacefully. The Grays state that their breeding program will repopulate the Earth after the approaching cataclysm that makes the planet uninhabitable for our type of life. The alien agenda, Jacobs believes, has three stages—"gradual, accelerated, and sudden." When his book came out back in the 1980s, Jacobs believed we were in the accelerated phase, which apparently has continued until this time.

Under hypnosis, abductees report that they are being trained to operate the Grays' saucers - to herd masses of people, like frightened sheep, into them, when the moment is right for the "sudden" phase. The accounts compiled in abductee Karla Turner's *Into the Fringe: A True Story of Alien Abduction (1992)* and *Taken: Inside the Alien-Human Agenda* (1994) support Jacobs' views. She recounts one dreamlike out-of-body experience where she was shown the aliens' plans for the future. She learned that the current human species is the result of genetic manipulation by these aliens in the past. Now they seek to engineer a new species for the time ahead. The aliens plan a "deception... through exploitation and manipulation of global events, including weather phenomenon, to make us believe the planet is in imminent danger of cataclysm and destruction." At this point, "when they show themselves openly and offer to save us in some way, we will be willing to take their help, even if it means giving up our birthright" and accepting "subjugation."

Turner also explores the aliens' ability to create an "artificially induced virtual-reality scenario (VRS), an externally introduced event, that to the witness is practically indistinguishable from objective reality. The person may experience a situation with full sensory input and react with genuine physical and emotional responses, although in 'reality' the person may be lying immobile on an exam table, or sitting attached to some alien apparatus, or even asleep in bed with no outward sign of disturbance."

Jacobs suspects the visitors' often nonsensical behavior is a cunning way of disguising their hideously grim intent. Like cunning cartoon villains, the visitors have used our own propensity for disbelief to render us defenseless to their agenda, which is the incipient takeover of the Earth. One abductee reports, "After The Change, there will be only one form of government: The insectile aliens will be in complete control. There will be no necessity to continue national governments. There will be 'one system' and 'one goal.'" Jacobs ends on a note of dread: "We now know the alarming dimensions of the alien agenda and its goals. . . . I do not think about the future with much hope. When I was a child, I had a future with much hope. . . . Now I fear for the future of my own children."

Nothing about the Greys suggests they belong to another civilization like our own, with a particular culture and history. They seem to exist entirely in relationship to us - a bit like machines or biological robots with a reduced sense of individual identity. One theory is that they are clones from an extraterrestrial race that lost its capacity to reproduce long ago. That is why they seek to extract our genetic material and create hybrids. It is the only way they can perpetuate themselves. As clones, the Greys may have reproduced themselves so many times that they lost any sense of their original identity or personality, like faded Xerox copies. Another theory is that they are postmodern versions of ancient elemental beings known from folktales and fairytales, such as goblins or gnomes. As imaginal projections, such entities take different forms that correspond with our level of social and technological evolution. The occult philosopher Rudolf Steiner (1861 - 1925) called such super-sensible beings "root spirits" that live within the Earth. Some of his descriptions resonate with modern abduction accounts:

"Anyone who gets to the stage of experiencing his dreams in full consciousness on falling asleep is well acquainted with the gnomes," Steiner wrote. "For somebody unprepared, the experience would be an alarming one: at the moment of falling asleep, he would behold a whole host of goblins coming towards him. . . . The form in which they would appear would actually be reflections, images of all the qualities in the individual concerned that work as forces of destruction. He would perceive all the destructive forces within him, all that continually destroys."

The abduction phenomenon occurs at a different level of consciousness than the waking state we experience during a normal day. It takes place in a twilight reality, a subliminal, hypnagogic state like that between sleep and waking. There is a quality of quantum indeterminacy about all of it. This may extend to manifestations that we might think must be purely material—such as the Roswell incident of the crashed "flying disc," or the many government reports and semiofficial statements that reveal nothing, and perhaps conceal nothing as well. In books and on Internet sites, former officials in the military or government admit to taking part in an organized cover-up of alien activity, while offering little convincing evidence. Is it conceivable that even these high-level political and military figures collude with the aliens - to the point of signing Faustian contracts - yet themselves flicker in and out of awareness of what they are doing?

It seems that the entire phenomena - the abductions, the crashed saucers, the recovered bodies, the transferred technology - hovers on the boundary between real and imaginary, much like a quantum "wavicle" or Schroedinger's infamous cat. It is difficult to imagine - quite hard to believe - that we may actually be approaching a threshold event, an ecological or military catastrophe, where these cartoon-like bug-eyed aliens suddenly step out of the shadows, make a public appearance and offer us a form of salvation through subjugation (a bargain you should definitely not accept!). Yet that is what the abduction narrative seems to be warning us. It is equally possible, however, that, as a manifestation of the paradoxical "daimonic reality" Harpur describes, this final culmination, despite all of the foreshadowing, will never arrive in such dramatic fashion. What future event undergoes "the formality of actually occurring" may depend on the choice made by human consciousness - each of us individually and all of us collectively - as to which future we draw into manifestation, or which branching timeline we choose, like the monkeys we are, to climb along.

4. BRANCHING TIMELINES AND FREQUENCY SHIFTS

The theory that what we take to be reality is actually a degraded simulacrum - that the truth of the spiritual or divine realm is intentionally disguised and hidden from us - comes from Gnosticism. The Gnostics were not a heretical sect of Christianity but holders of the ancient Mystery School teachings from the Classical world. In their cosmology, the goddess Sophia lived at the center of the universe, the Pleroma. According to this myth, Sophia began to have dreams of the Earth, this beautiful blue-green world. She became so captivated by her dream that she descended from the Pleroma to become the materialized body of the Earth, losing all consciousness of herself in the process.

Sophia's fall into matter caused ripples in the fabric of space-time, little rips and tears in it, and through these gaps, a group of evil beings, the Archons, entered this reality, descending with her as she became the Earth. These beings, under their leader, the Demiurge, seek to imprison the human inhabitants of Earth, Sophia's children, into a false reality governed by unconsciousness and fear. Human fear and slavish devotion - the energy of our attention - is "food" for them. They try to keep us in a dependent state so we keep feeding them.

The Demiurge pretends to be God, and the Archons devise false religious teachings, such as Judaism and Christianity, that cunningly delude human beings into worshipping them, instead of using their inner powers to liberate themselves. In the Gnostic version of Genesis, the serpent in the Garden of Eden is actually Christ, bringing knowledge to humans, seeking to liberate them from the wicked Demiurge who keeps us in ignorance.

Many modern occult thinkers belong to the Gnostic tradition. These thinkers tend to believe that the modern phenomenon of UFOs and alien abductions may be the continuation of a very ancient story, that of the Archons, devious off-planet entities whose goal is to subvert humanity's spiritual evolution and absorb our consciousness and etheric energy to fulfill their own goals. On the opposite side, there are UFO supporters like Steven Greer, who helped to spearhead the Disclosure Project, getting military personnel to tell of their encounters with UFOs and alien craft.

Greer seems to believe that the military, rather than aliens, are responsible for all of the malevolent abductions - the myriad accounts involving unwanted surgical procedures, removal of eggs and sperm, deviant sexuality, various forms of mind control and psychological terrorism. "There's not a shred of evidence that these UFOs or the life-forms behind them are a threat or hostile to us," Greer says. "There is a lot of evidence that some rogue military projects have done foolish and dangerous things that have been aggressive toward them. ... I have no doubt that the outcome will be peaceful, that these technologies will completely rehabilitate Earth's fortunes and environment, and eliminate poverty. And it will happen in our lifetimes." This odd stance, ignoring reams of horrible abduction accounts, has led others within the UFO community to suspect that Greer, himself, is part of the many layers of disinformation that seem to permeate the UFO and abduction phenomenon, making it so difficult to separate signal from noise.

I find elements of the Gnostic worldview — presented by John Lamb Lash in *Not In His Image* (2006), among other authors — to be very compelling. Lash looks at the difference between the Dead Sea Scrolls and the Gnostic Gospels of Nag Hammadi, both discovered in caves just after World War Two. The Dead Sea Scrolls are early examples of Jewish scripture, with God or the demiurge remaining the traditional patriarchal authority figure, based on contact with off-planet forces. The Gnostic Gospels are radically different, promoting a mysticism based on direct personal knowledge of divinity. We are meant to "open the door" for ourselves. For instance, in The Gospel of Thomas, Christ says, "One who seeks will find, and for [one who knocks] it will be opened."

Christianity as well as Judaism and Islam are, from the Gnostic point of view, intentionally deviated systems. They are traps designed by the Archons to imprison us. They force human beings to surrender their sovereignty and look for transcendence somewhere up above, in a distant Heaven. "Salvation" or "redemption" is not a result of direct realization or esoteric development. It comes through faith and devotion - as well as, for Christians, belief in Christ's divinity.

If those aliens or Archons who appear in abduction accounts emanate from a different dimension of space-time, they could pass backwards and forwards through time, as we do through space. If that is the case, we may consider that much of what we experience collectively - the procession of historical and geopolitical events - could have been tampered with or engineered by these hyper-dimensional entities to bring about results they desire.

While this idea may make us feel powerless and helpless at first, we can take comfort in the thought that there may be many levels of consciousness as well as more advanced entities - cosmic buddhas, divine Dakins - floating through the multi-verse. As we help ourselves, we may also be able to receive help and support from beings that support us and want to see humanity evolve and thrive. As we will discuss in a bit, this is the message I received from my study of the crop circles.

On his website, Veil of Reality, Bernhard Guenther has written at length about what he calls the "Hyperdimensional Matrix Control System" devised to prevent humanity from liberating itself and moving toward peace, harmony, and collective realization. He builds on other thinkers such as Laura Knight-Jadczyk, author of *High Strangeness* (2005). She channels entities called the Cassiopeans, who claim to be us from the future (the same claim is made by the channeled entity Bashar, whose ideas I sometimes find deliriously enticing). UFOlogist Jacques Vallee wrote, "I believe there is a system around us that *transcends time as it transcends space*. The system may well be able to locate itself in outer space, but its manifestations are *not spacecraft in the ordinary 'nuts and bolts' sense*. The UFOs are physical manifestations that cannot be understood apart from their psychic and symbolic reality. What we see in effect here is not an alien invasion. It is *a control system* which acts on humans and *uses* humans."

If we accept provisionally the idea of a "hyper-dimensional matrix" or occult control system, orchestrated by entities from a different spacetime dimension, I believe this helps us make sense of many things that remain bizarre and confusing otherwise. Examples include Trump's election and the mind-controlling power of Fox

News, which puts people into a hypnotized state. Another example is 9-11, the attack on the World Trade Centers. I won't go too far down that particular wormhole, but there are many incongruous details around the events of that day (even the date itself seems an obvious signal). It seems impossible to comprehend logically, from a purely materialist point of view. What if the various layers of murkiness are actually part of an occult plan, a hyper-dimensional operation requiring human sacrifice and mass chaos to anchor a particular frequency into the world?

Let's venture an admittedly as-of-yet unprovable hypothesis: The collective consciousness of contemporary humanity has been shaped, over many centuries, by these other-worldly intruders. These alien visitors have infiltrated our world, influencing or even creating our belief structures. They have intentionally distorted the truth in order to keep us under their control. They have done this for their own purposes, which we may be able to understand, to some extent, by carefully surveying the evidence and applying both reason and intuition. There is also a sense of increasingly accelerated activity - as if they are preparing for something like a harvesting or reaping of their efforts.

From this perspective, we might look at events like the Roswell crash in a different light. The entire event happened - but it happened in an in-between realm, hovering on the boundary between real and imaginal. However, as we enter an increasingly dreamlike reality - undergoing a collective phase-shift in the transition to the 6th Sun, a Sun of Darkness, the event becomes increasingly concretized and demonstrably "real." In all probability, such crashes and recoveries were not accidents. it is absurd to think that aliens with aerospace technologies seemingly light years ahead of our own would be so unskillful as to crash their physical crafts. Most likely, such episodes are engineered by these hyper-dimensional intruders at particular historical junctures to shape the timeline toward the particular goal they are seeking.

Knight-Jadczyk writes: "What we see now in terms of the diminishing resources of our planet, the intensified UV bombardment of our atmosphere, is not an "unfortunate but inevitable byproduct of industrialization": it is part of the deliberate, covert effort of the Negative hierarchy to prepare the biochemical and electrical composition of this planet for negative polarization." I find this a plausible theory, which echoes ideas from many other visionaries, including the great scientist and psychedelic explorer John Lilly. Through his explorations of LSD and ketamine in isolation tanks, Lilly arrived at the theory that a "solid-state intelligence," purely technological consciousness, was working against humanity, goading us on to annihilate the organic biosphere to create the conditions for a mechanized future reality that will be nonhuman and silicon-based.

In his essay, "Timeline-Reality Split, Frequency Vibration, and the Hidden Forces of Life," Guenther proposes we are going to see an increasing bifurcation between humans at different levels of consciousness, and that, eventually, there will be a kind of split or separation onto different "timelines" as we take entirely different evolutionary paths. This is something expressed by many occult thinkers in different ways. Guenther proposes the most important element in this time of accelerating change is to focus on our own embodiment, which means the integration of the masculine and feminine polarities within ourselves. He also proposes accepting the existence of evil as necessary for the divine plan, and overcoming any naive idea of trying to "save the world," which immediately reinforces duality.

Lisa Renee, a well known channeler and psychic, foresees a "forthcoming split occurring between timelines which govern our continued consciousness (energy) expression on the earth plane as it is moving into future time." For Renee, the choice of which timeline to follow lies within each individual, depending on their level of inner development. The positive side of this bifurcation will be realized through the "attraction of gathering people" who "begin to form reality bubbles of shared belief systems that will be contained throughout the land mass and spread to different locations across the globe. As similar resonance attracts groups to form community and collaboration, these areas on the earth of matched frequency will be increasingly synchronized." Articulations like this one can be useful and satisfying to contemplate, as long as one is careful not to become fixated on any particular outcome or viewpoint.

Rudolf Steiner, the extraordinary visionary who founded Anthroposophy, claimed that the mission of his life on Earth was to bring the knowledge of reincarnation back to the modern West. This knowledge had been lost to us thousands of years ago, due to Judeo-Christian conditioning. He wrote a series of books, titled *Karmic Relationships*, where he traced different significant historical and cultural figures through their past lives - much as Tibetan Buddhism recognize certain Lamas as reincarnations, returning in new bodies. Steiner also said that not only human beings, but the Earth as a whole, incarnates again and again, taking different forms that reflect different stages in the evolution of consciousness of human beings, plants, animals, and even minerals.

According to Steiner, this is currently the fourth incarnation of the Earth, approaching the apotheosis or metamorphosis into the fifth incarnation. In this present stage, humans possess four "bodies" which Steiner calls the physical body, the Ether Body, the Astral Body, and the "I" or the Ego. The I or the Ego is the new body we have attained in this fourth world. As we move toward the next incarnation of the Earth, we slowly attain a fifth body, which he called the "Spirit Self." At this stage, humans struggle because the "I" or Ego is still relatively weak. The Ego has to contend with all of the intense cravings and desires that pour into us from the Astral World, from the vast multitude of disembodied spirits who yearn to experience the sensorial world. This leads to addictive, compulsive, and self-destructive patterns of behavior. As the I or Ego becomes strong and supple enough to handle these cravings, we begin to create a new body, the Spirit Self, which represents the part of the Astral Body we have transformed and, in a sense, tamed. Just as this fourth world focused on the development of the I or Ego, the fifth incarnation will focus on the development of the Spirit Self and our ability to master the forces of the astral world.

Steiner also wrote, every time the Earth undergoes such a metamorphosis, many human souls will not have reached the level of development that will allow them to be part of the new incarnation. These souls must follow an alternative evolutionary trajectory. Steiner even talks about certain degraded or evil portions of humanity eventually becoming part of a new "moon" that goes off on a deviant path. Once again, I am not suggesting we take Steiner's articulation literally as "Holy Writ." I find it helpful and instructive to consider many different articulations of the esoteric or occult cosmology. By layering them, one begins to fathom a different pattern of information or knowledge. It is almost like learning how to listen to a new kind of music, which seems quite strange at first, until you get used to it.

I find that much of Steiner's occult cosmology meshes sensibly with the ongoing revelation of the UFO and alien influence in our world. At least, it gives me a scaffolding or map for understanding this cosmological saga or puzzle, which otherwise seems quite baffling. Steiner also stated that, in the 21st Century, humanity, as a whole, would be "crossing the threshold" into the spiritual world, and that the occult being he called "Ahriman" would incarnate into the Earth in this century, as part of this process.

As esoteric Christian thinker, Steiner understood the incarnation of the Christ as a crucial event in humanity's spiritual evolution. As part of his metaphysical system, he expanded the idea of the singular Devil described in the Bible. He proposed, instead, that a number of different occult beings - types or classes of spirits - continuously work upon humanity, seeking to divert or deviate us from our proper path of development. He differentiated the two main types of deviant spirits by the names of Lucifer and Ahriman. For Steiner, Christ's incarnation didn't "save" the souls of the faithful. Instead, he provided a model, showing how to balance between these different occult forces - a template we can follow if we wish to develop ourselves.

Luciferic spirits are beings that have, in some ways, evolved much farther than human beings. They have developed to a point where they can no longer take physical bodies themselves. They are not evil beings, but perhaps slightly amoral. They have a tendency to make us unhinged.

The term "Lucifer" literally means "light bringer," and Steiner named his magazine, Lucifer Gnosis. Luciferic spirits carry us upward toward beauty, glamor, artistic and intellectual accomplishment - but also toward pride, haughtiness, and arrogance. They pull us away from the Earth. In fact, these Luciferic beings can only further their own evolution by making an alliance with a human being, trading their inspiration and power for the humbling and grounding experience of human embodiment. The word "genius" originally comes from Genie, akin to the Arabic word *Djinn*. In the ancient world, men understood that their genius came from a power outside of themselves, through building a relationship or alliance with a supersensible being, a djinn, genie, or daemon.

Ahrimanic spirits, on other hand, seek to pull us downward toward materiality, sterility, rationality, material technologies, entropy and death - not just physical death, but loss of soul and spiritual connection, which is far worse. As I noted, Steiner prophesied that the Ahrimanic forces would reach their ascendancy in the Twenty-first Century, with a literal incarnation of Ahriman occurring in this time, in the Earthly material realm. Personally, I foresee the approach of this Ahrimanic incarnation in the race to develop a generalized Artificial Intelligence - a super-rational self-aware entity - on the one hand, and in the alien abduction saga on the other. The soulless, unfeeling Greys seem to be Ahrimanic entities who seem to be working frantically to break through the dimensional gateway so they can fully enter into our dimension, incarnating through hybridization.

I realize this is a lot to assimilate. There is a suggestion in Steiner's work - also found in channelled transmissions like Bashar or Knight-Jadczyk's Cassiopeans - that the metamorphosis we are undergoing will eventually lead us to a level of "supersensible" existence where we are no longer limited to physical bodies. This is also something earnestly discussed, from a different angle, by technologists like Google Director Ray Kurzweil. In *The Singularity is Near*, Kurzweil envisions a near future where we will be able to upload our consciousness to digital networks as a means of overcoming mortality. In fact, transhumanist philosophers like Nick Bostrom theorize that it is very probable we already live inside of a simulated reality that must exist as software running in some kind of alien supercomputer. I find it fascinating that technologists and engineers have arrived at a vision of the future that conjures the religious vision of a "Last Judgement" followed by an eternal Heaven, or "ascendance" into a noncorporeal, spiritualized state of being.

William Irwin Thompson, a cultural critic with a metaphysical viewpoint and a deep interest in Steiner's ideas, has proposed that the "evolutionary crisis of our time is the disintegration of the physical plane and the animal body as the vehicle for the incarnation of human beings. This is happening through declining fertility caused by chemical pollution in the environment and from all kinds of electromagnetic pollution from the invisible electromagnetic fields that surround us ... We are at a new catastrophe bifurcation in human evolution, one in which we have to reconfront the demonic and the astral plane and learn again how to tell the difference between the spiritual and the psychic." I agree with Thompson that, as we emerge from the flat materialist paradigm, many of us struggle to differentiate between ambiguous psychic experience (like abductions or various entity contact experiences in shamanic trance) and what is actually enlightening or healthy for our development.

Thompson postulates that the future vehicle of incarnation will not be a separate organic body but perhaps something more like a lattice or network. "When the new heaven comes down, the Earth is transformed and so the very nature of physical matter is transformed," he writes in *Coming into Being*. While I find these ideas fascinating, my personal belief and intuition is that we have much more work to accomplish in this physical realm before we can successfully "graduate" to a supersensible or hyper-dimensional next-level of reality. If we are going to "ascend" in some sense, we first need to master our Earthly realm, our practice of embodiment. This requires the integration of our inner masculine and feminine, as well as finding the will and courage to dedicate and even sacrifice ourselves, if need be, for the redemption of our human community and the future flourishing of organic nature. It has, also, a social and political dimension that can't be ignored, requiring mature responsibility for the collective.

5 GALACTIC ORDERING DIRECTORATE

To recap what has been explored up to this point, we have considered the possibility that the current mass media focus on UFOs belongs to a larger process of disclosure. Over time, our culture is assimilating the disturbing yet tantalizing prospect that we regular receive visits from beings from other worlds - or even other-dimensional realities. Factions within the military appear to be well aware that this is happening and, according to historian Richard Dolan and other sources, they have undertaken extensive, highly classified efforts to understand the threat and to reverse-engineer the alien technology, which is far beyond our own. Along with the sightings of alien craft, we have many thousands of reported abduction accounts. Many of these are bizarre and troubling, suggesting that some faction among the aliens is seeking to forcibly create a hybrid human-alien species - although it is unclear if this is happening "literally" or in some dreamlike, hypnagogic reality. In these accounts, the aliens seem to take a kind of pleasure in tormenting their helpless victims in various cruel ways.

I have proposed that this phenomenon is best approached from an occult or esoteric perspective, because it challenges, and perhaps refutes, our obsolete Newtonian ideas of time, space, and matter. As Jaques Vallee wrote: "The UFOs are physical manifestations that cannot be understood apart from their psychic and symbolic reality. What we see in effect here is not an alien invasion. It is *a control system* which acts on humans and *uses* humans."

If these entities are in fact other-dimensional, they could move through time as we move through space. If they have indeed been with us, in different guises, throughout our evolutionary journey, they may have influenced and inflected our history, seeking to bring about a result that benefits them. There is an indication that they plan to fully incarnate into matter or to make use of some proportion of the human population for their own ends, at a time of chaos and catastrophe, which they are helping to orchestrate. It is also possible that this is a daemonic, trickster phenomenon that will always remain a little outside of a definitive, literal manifestation.

It is possible that we are on the verge of discovering that we are part of a vast ecology of alien, extraterrestrial, supersensible, and other-dimensional entities. Along with the malevolent Greys, there may also be benign and benevolent beings who wish us well and want to help us. These beings may have their own code of etiquette, laws or principles that define how they can engage or interact with us, at our current stage of development. This seems to me to be the message we can tease out from the crop circles, an ongoing phenomenon that also gets routinely ridiculed and dismissed.

I wrote at length about my experiences exploring the crop circles in *2012: The Return of Quetzalcoatl*. I lived in Glastonbury in the summer of 2002, visited the formations as they appeared and interviewed many researchers, self-confessed hoaxers, and other characters involved in the spectacle. Evidence suggests that at least some of the patterns are not made by humans. This includes the incredible scale and precision of the crop circles, as well as the changes in the plants within some of the formations, which have been studied by physicists. According to peer-reviewed papers published in science journals, the crop within the patterns often seems to be altered by some form of electromagnetic energy that spirals down from above. Mysterious "balls of light" have been frequently observed floating above the patterns.

I was open-minded but skeptical about the crop circles at first. But as I explored them for myself, I experienced many uncanny synchronicities and anomalies. Some of the patterns reference the Mayan Tzolkin calendar and a few make particular reference to aliens and ETs. One very large, dramatic and precisely rendered formation from 2002 showed an image of a typical Grey holding a computer disk. Inscribed on the disk was a coded message, in ASCII, that said, in part, "Beware the bearers of FALSE gifts & their BROKEN PROMISES... There is GOOD out there. We OPpose DECEPTION." Taken at face value, this message appears to be a warning about the Greys, and also seems to suggest that these beings are giving us "false gifts," perhaps in the form of technology (like the computer disk), as part of a greater scheme to swindle us.

This is one of the few direct written messages to be found among the patterns, which tend to explore sacred geometries and reference the ancient stone circles and megalithic structures of the Neolithic period, which is well represented in that area of England by Stonehenge, Silbury Hill and Avebury. Many of them refer to the ancient problem in geometry known as "squaring the circle" - creating a circle and square with an equal circumference. There is no simple mathematical solution to this problem, which was known to symbolize the integration of Heaven and Earth. Heaven is classically represented by the circle; Earth by the square. Other patterns seem to offer blueprints for energy technologies we might build. Some have been interpreted as suggesting the existence of a "galactic federation" of some sort, waiting in the wings.

I found the crop circles, much like psychedelics, to be "nonspecific psychic amplifiers." The phenomenon seemed subtly responsive to the mindset you brought to it. If you were skeptical, you would find evidence to support your skepticism. If you were a conspiracy theorist, you would encounter military intelligence at the sites, while black helicopters circled overhead. If you were a fluffy New Ager, you might see light beings and angels fluttering around the patterns and receive messages of ascension from them.

It was also extremely difficult, if not impossible, to verify that any particular formation was either "real" (made by some nonhuman agency) or "fake" (constructed by hoaxers or self-proclaimed crop artists). A friend of mine wrote an entire treatise on one pattern - a circling double helix - that had complex mathematical codes embedded in it. He thought its complexity was beyond human ingenuity. Later he received images that seemed to reveal it was made by crop artists, after all. The experience shook his confidence. Yet later we found more evidence that humans could not have made it.

As I became enmeshed in the phenomenon, I found I couldn't sleep at night as I went over all of the contradictory evidence regarding particular patterns and the crop circles as a whole. Finally, I had an "aha" moment. I realized the entire phenomenon was designed to act like those proverbs in Zen, called koans, which monks meditate on for many years before they attain illumination. Questions like, "What is the sound of one hand clapping?" - a classic Zen koan - can break apart our intellectual need for rational explanation and shatter our faith in linear cause and effect. The crop circles seemed to be indicating that the nature of reality is inherently paradoxical. On some level, dualities like "real" and "fake," cause and effect, exist only in the human mind.

Friedrich Nietzsche reached a similar conclusion in the late 19th Century: "In the "in-itself " there is nothing of "causal connections," of "necessity," or of "psychological non-freedom"; there the effect does *not* follow the cause, there is no rule or "law." It is *we* alone who have devised cause, sequence, for-each-other, relativity, constraint, number, law, freedom, motive, and purpose; and when we project and mix this symbol world into things as if it existed "in itself," we act once more as we have always acted—*mythologically,"* he wrote in *Beyond Good and Evil*.

In the course of writing *2012: The Return of Quetzalcoatl*, I kept returning to Nietzsche, who somehow reached a profound understanding of the invisible biases hidden within our language and thought, even without access to psychedelics. In his work, he relentlessly exposed these biases. His speculations meshed with my findings as I explored esoteric subject matter such prophecies, crop circles, psychic phenomena, and alien abductions. I would contemplate Nietzche's provocations, such as this one: "Why couldn't the world *that concerns us*—be a fiction? And if somebody asked,"but to be a fiction there surely belongs an author?"—couldn't one answer simply: why? Doesn't this "belongs" perhaps belong to the fiction, too?"

What I gleaned from my study of the crop formations is that there are extra- as well as infra-terrestrial and other-dimensional forces working with and for humanity, as well as those working against us. The technique for contacting these more benevolent forces requires, I believe, attaining a heightened state of humble receptivity, on the one hand, while on the other hand, finding an appropriate, active way to reach out toward them. In other words, melding the feminine, receptive, and masculine, active, aspects of ourselves in an occult investigation.

As Rudolf Steiner explored in depth in books like *How to Know Higher Worlds* and *An Outline of Esoteric Science*, when it comes to navigating what he called the "supersensible" realms, we are always in danger of projecting our shadow material and receiving contacts that mirror and amplify our darker aspects. In the individual's journey toward initiation, in fact, such an episode is inevitable, and invariably frightening. Steiner calls it the encounter with the "Guardian of the Threshold." While we meet the Guardian as a separate being, this entity reflects all of our darkest and most malevolent aspects. Perhaps, if humanity and the Earth as a whole are undergoing a phase-state transition to a Sun of Darkness - a more psychic or lucid-dream-like level of reality, as the Aztecs foretold - we are currently confronting the Guardian of the Threshold collectively. It seems to be happening in politics, in the breakdown of our planetary ecology, in the exponentially malignant potential of futuristic technologies, and in the alien contact or abduction experiences that so many have recounted.

The thesis that we need to address the dangerous implications of the UFO and alien abduction phenomenon as a "psychic and symbolic reality," as well as a "control system which acts on humans and uses humans," contradicts certain trends in contemporary spiritual and New Age thought. These days, we find a strong tendency in many spiritual communities to focus single-mindedly on the power of positivity and affirmations of the light, based on ideas such as "The Law of Manifestation" or "The

Secret." The underlying belief is that each of us creates our own reality through our thoughts and intentions. Therefore, if we simply avoid anything dark or malevolent, nothing negative will be able to enter our field. But unfortunately, reality is not that simple, and this approach is a blatant form of spiritual bypassing.

Paul Levy explores the idea that modern Anglo-European culture is infected by what the Algonquins call "wetiko," a cannibalistic spirit driven by greed, excess, and selfish consumption. "Spiritual/New Age practitioners who endlessly affirm the light while ignoring the shadow" fall "under the spell of wetiko," he writes. By seeking to turn away from and hide their darkness, these practitioners unwittingly reinforce "the very evil from which they are fleeing. Looking away from darkness, thus keeping it unconscious, is what evil depends upon for its existence. If we unconsciously react … to evil by turning a blind eye toward it – "seeing no evil" – we are investing the darkness with power over us." The alternative is to permeate evil with awareness, "stalking" the shadow so we can catch and assimilate it. Carl Jung wrote, "One does not become enlightened by imagining figures of light, but by making the darkness conscious."

If the thesis developed in this essay has validity, then New Age spiritual practitioners will have to overcome their bypassing and confront the dark side of the psyche, reckoning with the occult control system. At the same time, political and ecological activists will need to interrogate their inveterate bias toward a purely materialist analysis, to acknowledge the existence of occult, hyper-dimensional, forces at work behind the scenes, influencing the course of events. And conspiracy theorists who believe in an incredibly evil, highly organized and intelligent cabal of human controllers working to bring about a New World Order surveillance society of enslavement will have to recognize that the controllers operating behind the scenes are not humans at all. Here and there, the Bible gets this right - as in Ephesians: "For we wrestle not against flesh and blood, but against principalities, against powers, against the rulers of the darkness of this world, against spiritual wickedness in high places." If we aren't aiming at the proper targets, we will never hit the mark.

Milk Hill, Wiltshire, 2001

ABOUT THE AUTHOR

Daniel Pinchbeck is the bestselling author of Breaking Open the Head, 2012: The Return of Quetzalcoatl, How Soon Is Now?,and When Plants Dream with Sophia Rokhlin. He co-founded the web magazine Reality Sandwich and the online platform Evolver.net. His essays and articles have appeared in publications including The New York Times, Esquire, Rolling Stone, and ArtForum. He was featured in the 2010 documentary, '2012: Time for Change', directed by Joao Amorim and produced by Mangusta Films. He speaks frequently at international conferences and festivals.

Printed in Great Britain
by Amazon

39563970R00030